This journal belongs to:

36456066R00061

Printed in Great Britain
by Amazon